I0815522

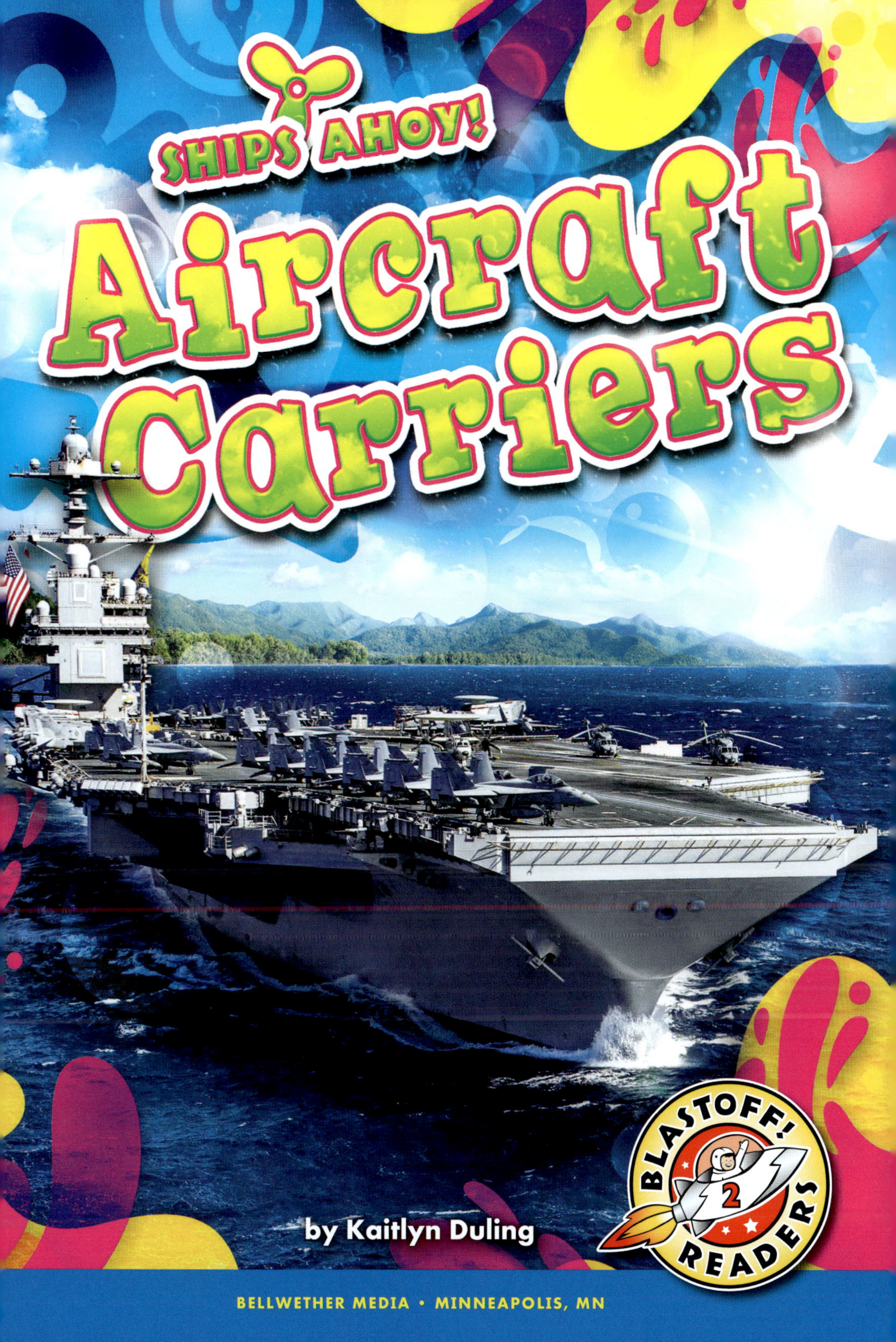
SHIPS AHOY!
Aircraft Carriers
by Kaitlyn Duling
BLASTOFF! 2 READERS
BELLWETHER MEDIA • MINNEAPOLIS, MN

Blastoff! Readers are carefully developed by literacy experts to build reading stamina and move students toward fluency by combining standards-based content with developmentally appropriate text.

Level 1 provides the most support through repetition of high-frequency words, light text, predictable sentence patterns, and strong visual support.

Level 2 offers early readers a bit more challenge through varied sentences, increased text load, and text-supportive special features.

Level 3 advances early-fluent readers toward fluency through increased text load, less reliance on photos, advancing concepts, longer sentences, and more complex special features.

★ **Blastoff! Universe**

Reading Level

Grade K

Grades 1–3

Grade 4

This edition first published in 2026 by Bellwether Media, Inc.

Library of Congress Cataloging-in-Publication Data

LC record for Aircraft Carriers available at: https://lccn.loc.gov/2025010710

Editor: Suzane Nguyen   Designer: Jeffrey Kollock

Printed in the United States of America, North Mankato, MN.

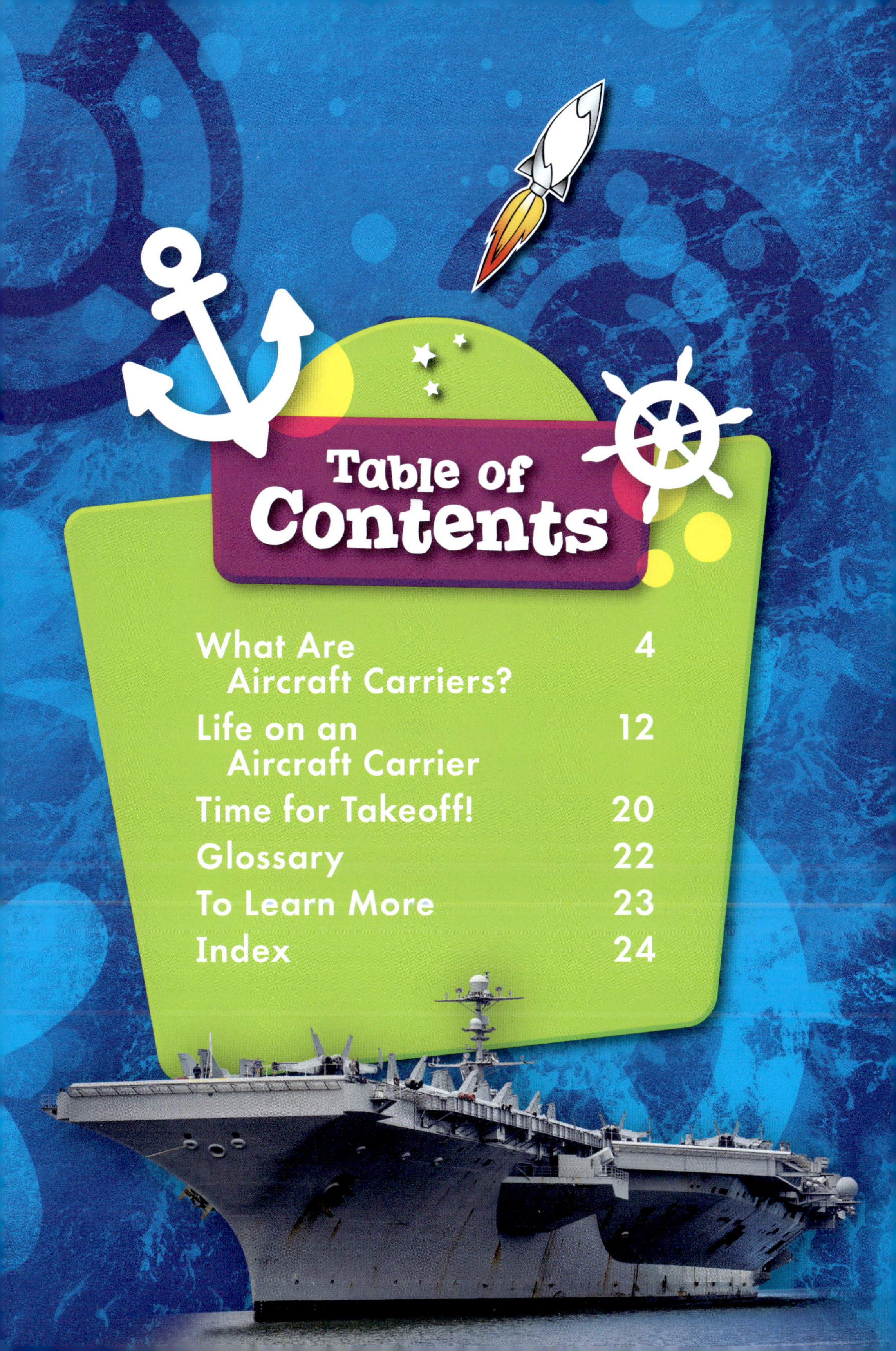

Table of Contents

What Are Aircraft Carriers?

Aircraft carriers are **warships**. They are used by the **military**.

Aircraft carriers are like airports at sea. Planes land and take off.

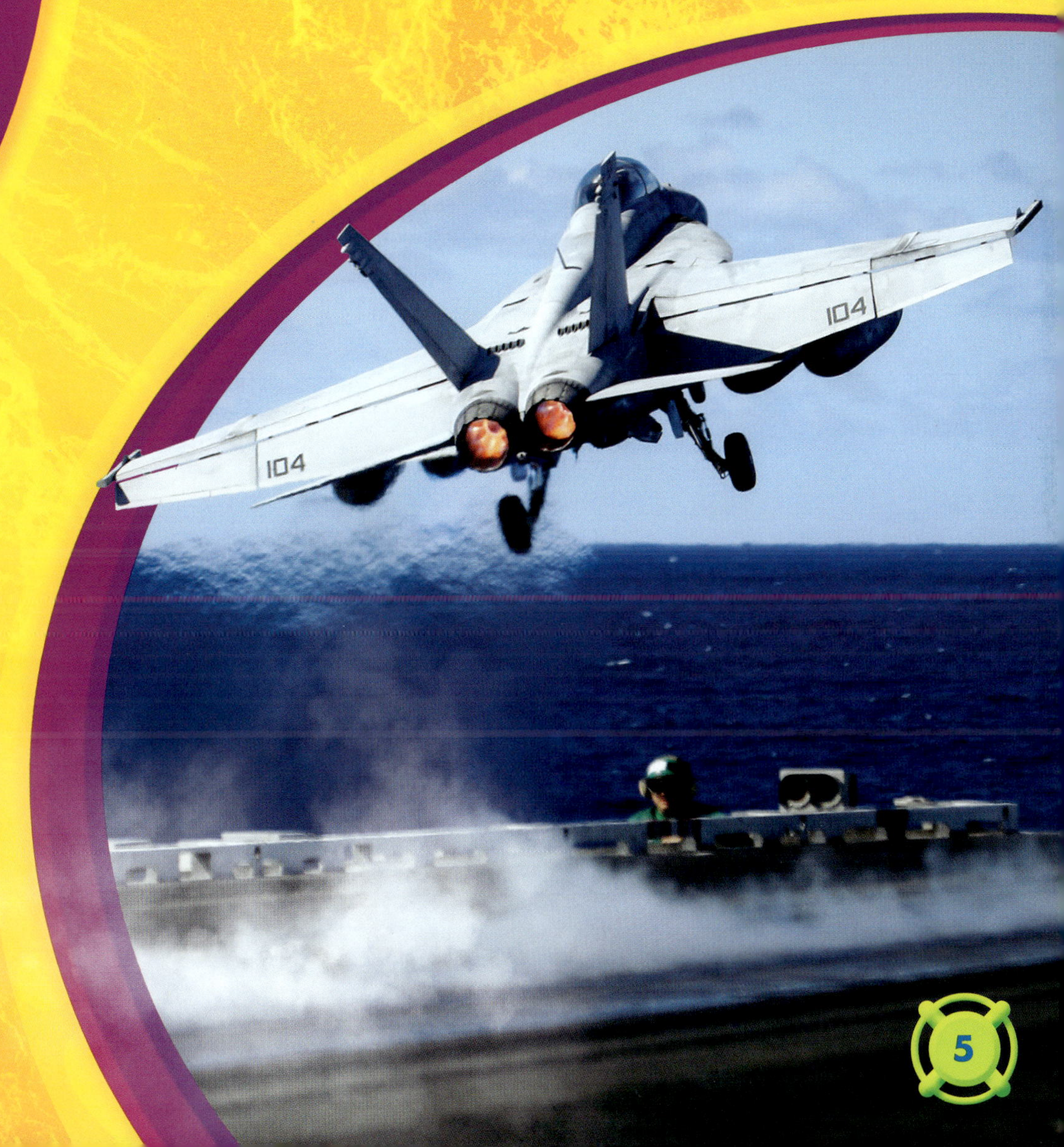

hull

hangar deck

Aircraft carriers have a **hull**.
It is the main part of the ship.
It helps the ship float.

Planes are stored in the hangar deck.

Catapults help planes take off from the **flight deck**.

Arresting wires help planes land. They catch **tailhooks** at the back of planes.

tailhook
501
arresting wires
flight deck

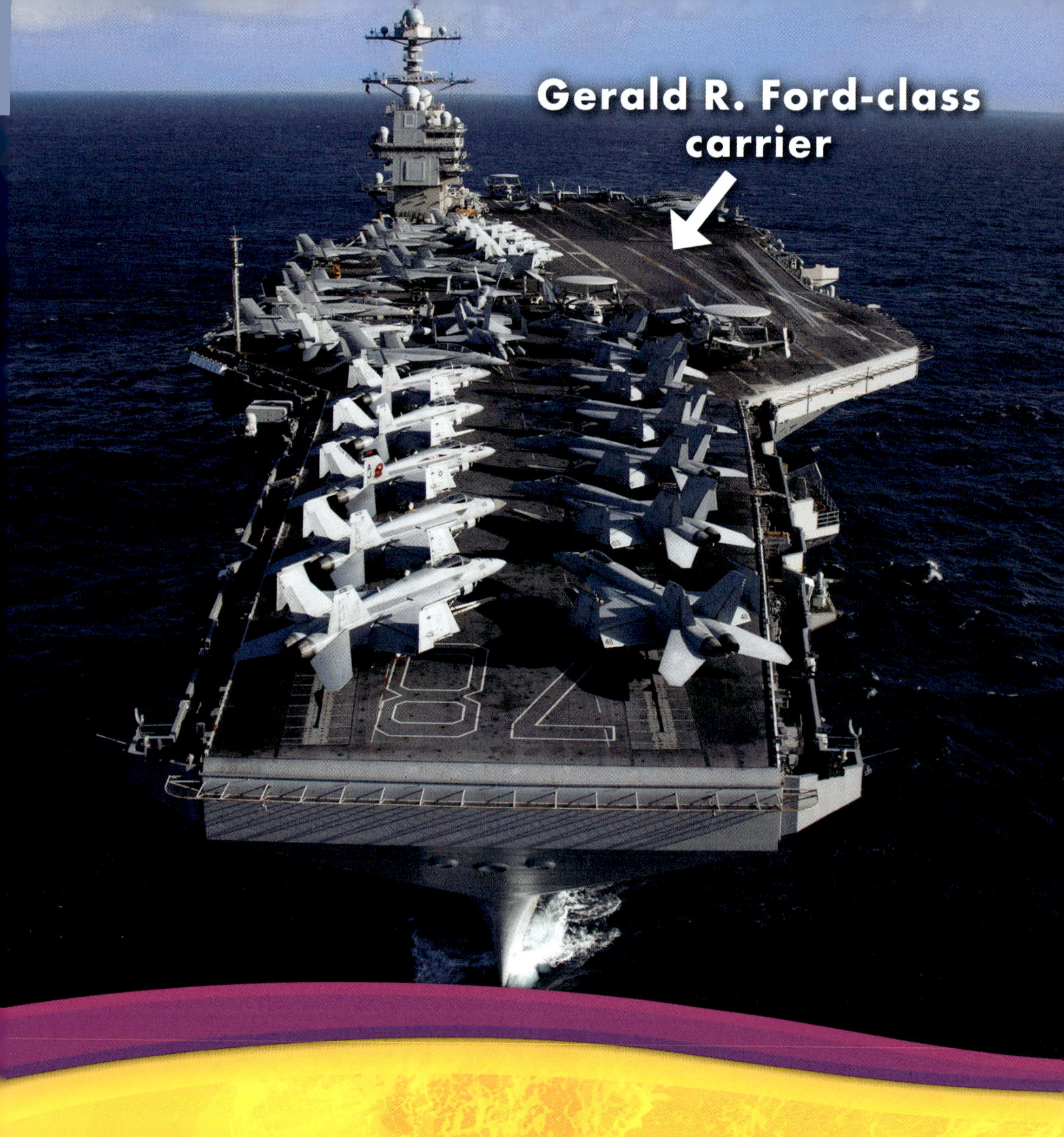

Gerald R. Ford-class ships are the biggest carriers. They can carry over 75 planes. Nimitz-class carriers usually hold 60 planes.

Escort carriers were used during World War II.

Life on an Aircraft Carrier

Aircraft carriers travel across the world. They can be at sea for months.

Four **propellers** move the ship. Aircraft carriers can move over 30 **knots** (35 miles or 55.6 kilometers per hour).

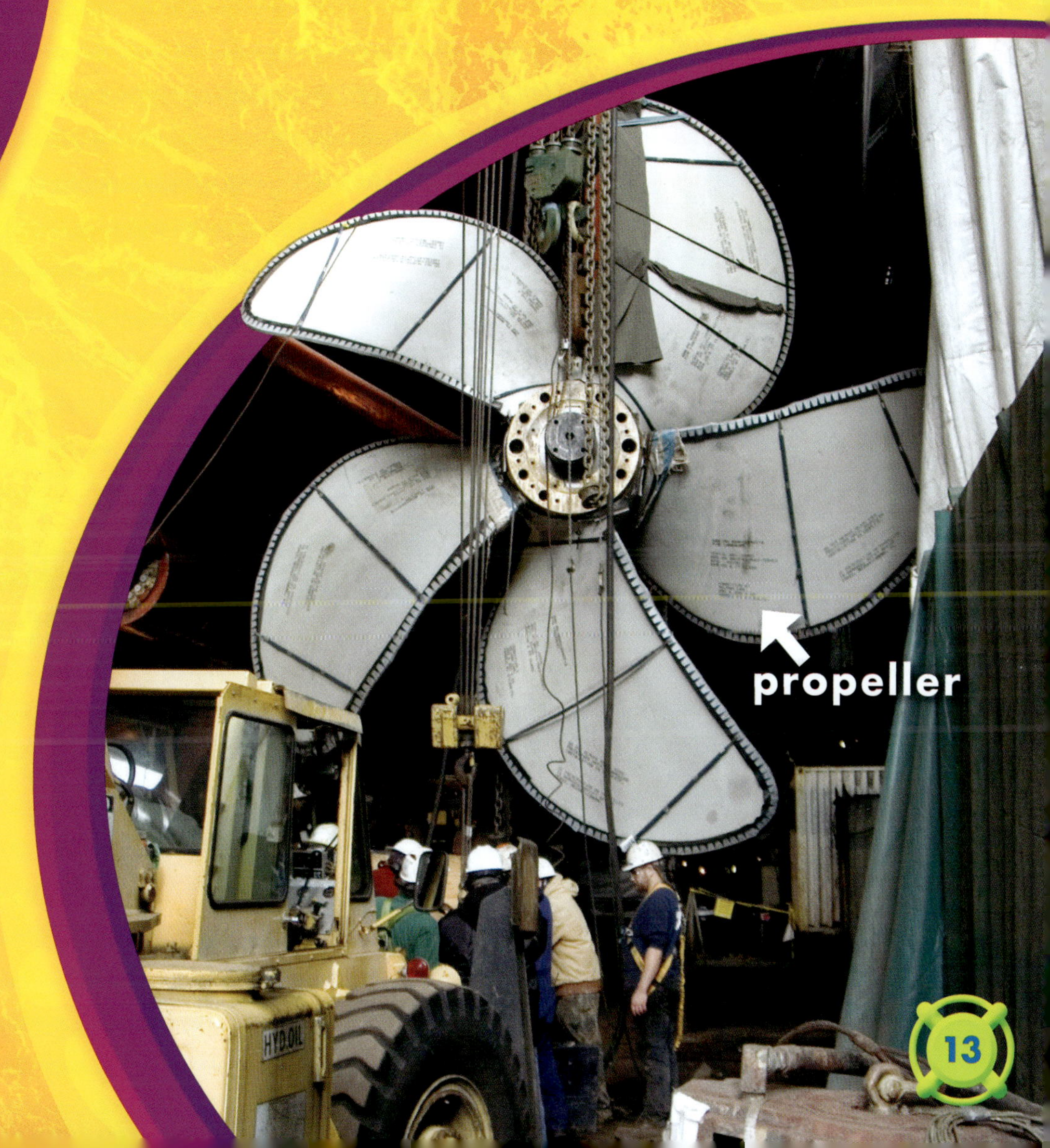

Aircraft carriers are like little cities. Many can hold up to 5,000 people.

Ship Stats

USS *George H. W. Bush* (CVN-77)

Size 1,092 feet (333 meters) long; 252 feet (77 meters) wide

Type Nimitz-class carrier

Top Speed more than 30 knots (35 miles or 55.6 kilometers per hour)

Purpose used by the United States Navy

Each crew member has a different job that helps the ship run.

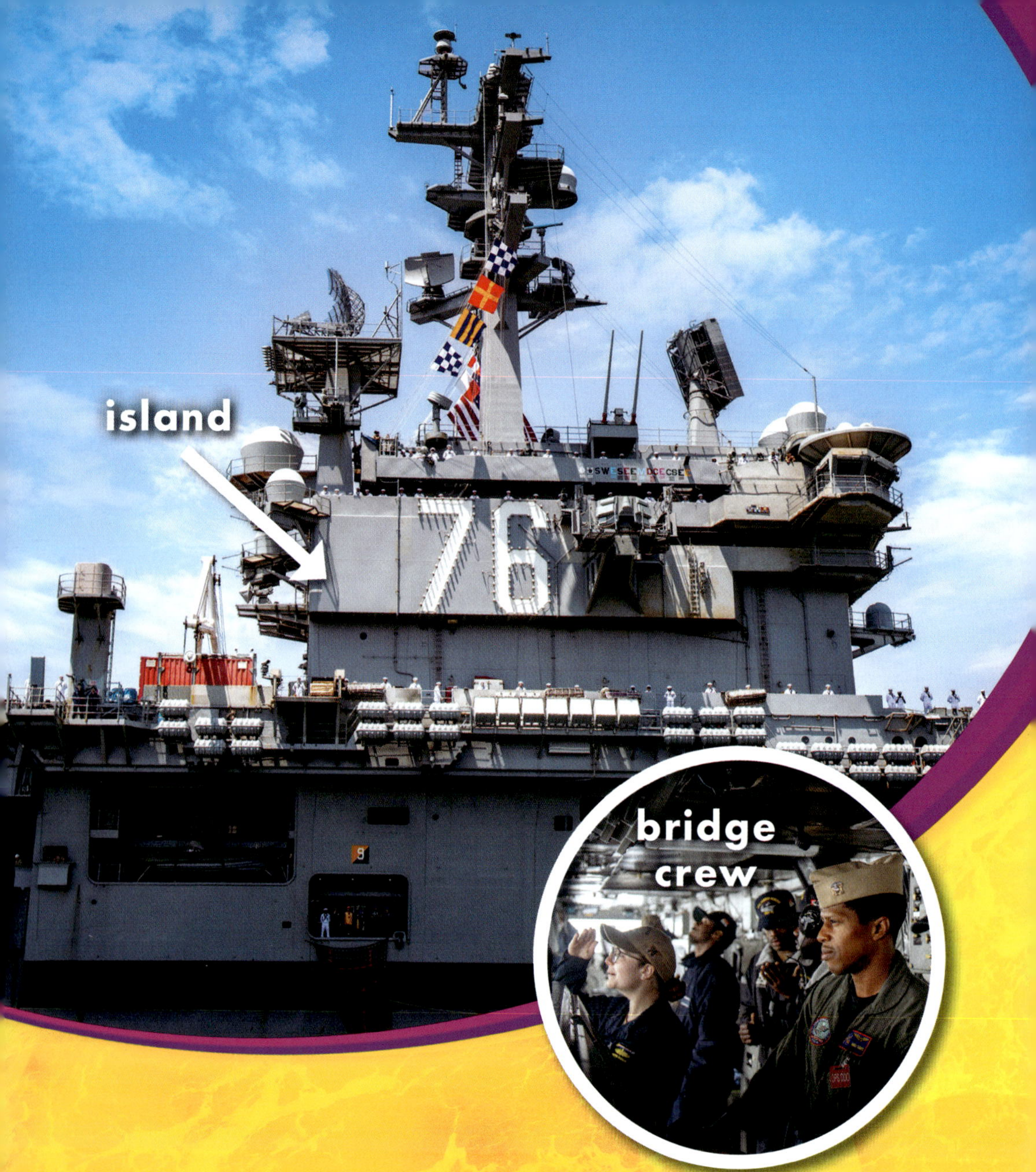

island

bridge crew

From the **island**, crew members guide pilots on flight decks.

Flight deck crew members help planes take off and land safely. **Bridge** crews steer ships.

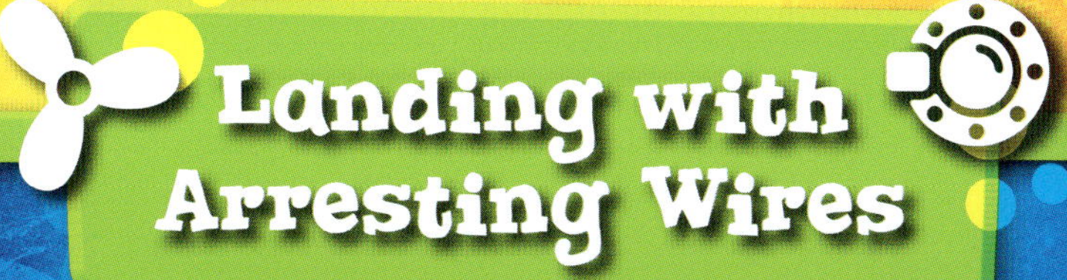

Landing with Arresting Wires

1

arresting wire

A machine with arresting wires stretches across the flight deck.

A plane lowers its tailhook.

The tailhook catches one of the wires.

The wires bring the plane to a stop.

Aircraft carriers have their own cooks, dentists, doctors, and barbers.

post office

shop

The ships even have shops and a post office!

Time for Takeoff!

Aircraft carriers help keep people safe. They bring planes closer to battle.

For the pilots and sailors on these ships, the sky is the limit!

Glossary

arresting wires—thick, steel cables used to rapidly slow an aircraft as it lands

bridge—a room where the ship is steered

catapults—devices used on aircraft carriers to help planes take off into the air

flight deck—the deck of an aircraft carrier where planes take off and land

hull—the body of a ship

island—the top part of an aircraft carrier where planes are directed to land and take off

knots—units of measurement used to explain the speed of a ship

military—the armed forces

propellers—parts of a ship that have blades that spin; propellers help a ship move through water.

tailhooks—hooks underneath planes that are used to catch onto arresting wires

warships—ships armed for war

To Learn More

AT THE LIBRARY

Bolte, Mari. *Aircraft Carriers in Action*. Minneapolis, Minn.: Lerner Publications, 2024.

Bradshaw, Eleanor. *Aircraft Carriers*. Buffalo, N.Y.: Enslow Publishing, 2025.

Grack, Rachel. *Curious About Aircraft Carriers*. Mankato, Minn.: Amicus Learning, 2025.

ON THE WEB

FACTSURFER

Factsurfer.com gives you a safe, fun way to find more information.

1. Go to www.factsurfer.com.
2. Enter "aircraft carriers" into the search box and click 🔍.
3. Select your book cover to see a list of related content.

Index

The images in this book are reproduced through the courtesy of: DVIDS/ DVIDS, front cover, pp. 1, 7 (bottom, hangar deck), 8, 9 (all), 10, 11 (Nimitz), 12, 14 (top, bottom), 15 (all), 16 (all), 17 (1, 3, 4), 18, 19 (all), 20, 21, 23; Jeff Whyte, p. 3; Photo Gallery, p. 4; Cameron, p. 5; GreenOak, p. 6; steve estvanik, p. 6 (hangar deck); Aerial-motion, p. 7 (top); U.S. Navy National Museum of Naval Aviation/ Wikimedia Commons, p. 11 (escort); Riley McDowell/ Wikimedia Commons, p. 11 (Gerald R. Ford); Matthew Dewitt/ Wikimedia Commons, p. 13; Stocktrek Images, Inc./ Alamy Stock Photo, p. 17 (2).